May, 2011

Deaths & Transfigurations

Deaths & Transfigurations: Poems

Paul Mariani

Engravings by Barry Moser

PARACLETE PRESS

BREWSTER, MASSACHUSETTS

Library of Congress Cataloging-in-Publication Data
Mariani, Paul L.
Deaths & transfigurations: poems / Paul Mariani. p. cm.
ISBN 1-55725-452-4
I. Title: Deaths and transfigurations. II. Title.
PS3563.A6543D43 2005
811'.54—dc22   2005006040

First Printing July, 2005

10 9 8 7 6 5 4 3 2 1

Text copyright 2005 by Paul Mariani

Interior design and engravings copyright 2005

by Barry Moser

ISBN 1-55725-452-4

Published by Paraclete Press

Brewster, Massachusetts

www.paracletepress.com

Printed in the United States of America

For Eileen

Unlike the Adirondacks or the Hudson River, Long Island Sound never stole the region's heart. It was always too close to New York City, too taken for granted, too practical in its uses—as a fishery, a transportation artery or a trash can. . . . What the Sound had, first and foremost, was people. . . . It was America's first urban sea, a kitchen sink for the industrial revolution, and an ecological witness to the rise of the suburbs after World War II. . . . Profound philosophical questions have emerged from this. If the Sound cannot be restored to what it was in the pre-European past—and no one thinks that is remotely possible—then what should it be? What is the optimum natural state in a system that has been overwhelmingly and permanently transformed by human presence?

—New York Times,
May 25, 2003

On the other hand, if the writer believes that our life is and will remain essentially mysterious, if he looks upon us as beings existing in a created order to whose laws we freely respond, then what he sees on the surface will be of interest to him only as he can go through it into an experience of mystery itself. His kind of fiction will always be pushing its own limits outward toward the limits of mystery. . . .

Flannery O'Connor

Chaff, straw, splinters of wood, weeds, and the sea-gluten,
Scum, scales from shining rocks, leaves of salt-lettuce, left by the tide,
Miles walking, the sound of breaking waves the other side of me. . . .

—WALT WHITMAN,
As I Ebb'd with the Ocean of Life

You may have a million dollars
Or you may drive a Cadillac.
You may have enough money
To buy anything you lack.
Well, don't care how rich you are,
Don't care what you're worth.
'Cause you know when it all comes down
You got to go back to Mother Earth.

It was an idea like any other. Probably the musical need,
after Macbeth *and* Don Juan, *to write a piece that begins*
in C minor and finishes in C major.

—RICHARD STRAUSS TO
FRIEDRICH ROSCH,
on the genesis of *Death and Transfiguration.*

Manshape, that shone
Sheer off, disseveral, a star, | death blots black out; nor mark
Is ány of him at áll so stárk
But vastness blurs and time | beats level. Enough! The Resurrection. . . .

—GERARD MANLEY HOPKINS,
That Nature is a Heraclitean Fire. . .

CONTENTS

ONE

TWO

ONE

Wasn't It Us You Were Seeking?

*All the while jumbled memories flirt out on their own, interrupting
the search for what we want, pestering: "Wasn't it us you were
seeking?" My heart strenuously waves these things off . . . until the
dim thing sought arrives at last, fresh from the depths.*

St. Augustine, *Confessions*

The lawns and mansions of old memories,
pale sea roses, the ululation of the willow trees.
These the mind strains after, and not the bully's gloat,
the barn, the bayonet gleaming like a tease,
pressed against a small boy's trembling throat.

"You wanted something other?" Something other.
Something lambent, like the memories of a mother.
The red eyes of the photo changed to brown,
the fret become a smile. Presto, another
mother altogether, the lady with a golden crown.

My sister, likewise spavined by life's events
(we are pilgrims here and have pitched our tents),
has written with the very best of wishes, and added
in a postscript only now: *It's been a tense
ten years refusing to mourn a mother ten years dead.*

"Wasn't it us you were seeking?" Clamant voices, out
of sorts with this submersion always into Memory and Doubt.
And now radar picks up human wreckage on the screen:
the dead, dredged up from the depths. And now a shout,
as they flop about the deck, raw, barnacled, obscene.

SOLAR ICE

The sudden shock of what you really are.
Early March. The tentative return of afternoons.
Saturday, and Mass again. The four.
All about swelling buds on beech & ash
& maples. Crocuses & snowdrops
trilling. Four months impacted ice at last
receding from the north side of the house,
and bobbing robins back & soon, soon, red-
winged blackbirds strutting on the lawn.
Soon too the sweet familiar groundswell
of peepers in the marshes. Reason
enough to melt the frozen heart.

Father lifted the host above his head & prayed:
a small white sun around which everything
seemed to coalesce, cohere & choir. But
as I raised my head, the thought
of some old insult likewise reared
its head, and in that instant the arctic
hatred flared, shutting out my world
& spring, along with, yes, my lovely wife & sons,
a no & no & yet another no, until I caught
myself refuse the proffered gift of Love

At once the host diminished to a tiny o:
an empty cipher, like some solar disc
imploding on itself. Only my precious
hate remained, the self-salt taste

of some old wound rubbed raw again,
a jagged O at the center of my world.
Ah, so this is it, I whistled through my teeth.
So this is hell, or some lovely ether
foretaste of it, alone at ninety north,
with darkness everywhere, & ice & ice
& ice & more ice on the way, and this
sweet abyss between myself & You.

New York, Christmas Eve, 1947

Snow falling darkly through darkening air.
Clip-clop of hooves on the cobbles below.
And the El up on Third, which will soon disappear.

Cries from the kitchen, cries everywhere.
A boy staring out into darkness below,
and snow falling darkly through darkening air.

Strains of White Christmas on the mothering air.
Winking lights, tinsel, toys, trains, mistletoe.
All, like the El, which will soon disappear.

Under the tree, in the reddish-blue glare,
a father lays train tracks in cottony snow,
while outside snow falls through the darkening air.

So much to do, the father's hands say. *So much to care
for, so much to fix*. And *oh* cries the boy, and *oh*
cries the little toy train, which will soon disappear.

And *oh*, cries the mother, in the cold kitchen out there,
though the boy thinks, *No one is crying*. And the snow
goes on falling through the darkening air,
on the El and the people, who will soon disappear.

STUDY IN BLACK & WHITE

Seven days a week, six till ten,
my father & I ran the Sinclair station
across from the county courthouse in Mineola.
Between customers I pored over *The Greatest
Story Ever Told* and *Amboy Dukes*

or worked out back among the jewelweed
& cinders, swabbing ballbearings in kerosene,
as I gloried in all I would in time become.
Late April, early May. The trees trembling
for the sun's caress. Hummed the papers

daily now of the noose grown tighter
round Dien Bien Phu. Black & white photos,
ghostly, dreamlike, with black-pajamed Viet
Minh sappers storming trenches, as elite
French paratroopers, bloodied, dazed, surrendered.

I was fourteen then, and stood ready
to take on evil wherever it should rear
its swollen head, not unlike the Archangel Michael
whose eight-foot statue hovered high above
the marble-white gothic altar at Corpus Christi.

Armored like the boy-god Augustus Imperator,
his bronze spear tormented the snarling serpent.
Only Butch, who lived behind the rusting diner
two doors down in his '41 wood-trimmed Chevy
wagon up on blocks, cared nothing

that the world my G.I. father had helped
make safe was already breaking down.
Butch spent himself poring over comics,
small ones, black & white, in which Wimpy did
forbidden things to Olive. In all weathers,

buried beneath a filthy army-issue olive blanket
flanked by whisky flasks & yellow newsprint,
the palsied body shook. But who knew anything
about Butch really? Where he came from or later
where he went? My father warned me away from him,

and when I asked him why, stared down at me
in utter disbelief. Could any son of his
be this goddamned stupid, he shook his head,
and still walk upright the face of God's sweet earth?
This was forty years ago, so that by now Butch

has surely returned to the same dust from which
we all once sprang, his end coming in some alley,
or one fine morning not waking from the backseat
of his car, carbon monoxide leaking into his final
dream of love to resurface here in memory defanged:

thinning hair slicked back, the toothless grin,
the right hand grasping the palsied left,
to hide the shaking as he sized you up, a face
you'd recognize in any bathroom mirror,
the poor forked mortal trembling thing itself.

EAST OF THE WHITESTONE

Where the East River fuses with the Sound
we rowed furiously against the insane waves,
Bob and I, and a third whose name I remember now
was Burnsey. We were fifteen then, and the talk
was all of girls, about whom we knew nothing, and this
Odyssean venture out beyond our accustomed
element our first glimpse into the fierce Sublime,
though surely it must have looked from atop
the Whitestone Bridge (which I have crossed a thousand
times since then) as though we were merely fishing
east of the Throgs Neck Bridge, which did not then exist,
unlike the river, which flowed on unremembering then
as now: cold, salt, dark, unplumbed, and unforgiving.

•

And Bob existed, as he worked his flimsy oar
against the waves that slammed the shaking gunwales.
And the other kid existed, though for the love of me
I can't remember him, and who just last week Bob told me
now was dead. And I existed, the one addressing you,
dear reader, disappearing bit by bit with each morseled day.
But that cold spring day in '55 I pulled the second oar
for all I was worth in both my shaking hands, glimpsing
three bodies bobbing face-down in those roiling waves.

•

For nearly thirty years I lost touch with Bob
through one fault or another, and know now I will
see the other boy no more. As for Bob, he lives in

California, miles inland, away from those vast Pacific
waters, and has a wife and two grown daughters. And Bob
is rich these days (very, you might say), though—for
what it's worth—when we met he pointed
to an empty suit he said could buy & sell us both.

•

But that's the now, whatever *now* means now.
Back then, soaked through & shaking, the three of us
did what we could to keep from being swamped
in the cold crosscurrents there between the River
and the Sound. And if we had gone down, no question
now of *who* was in the boat, or who finally *made* it
in any sense you'd care to take the word. And though the
dinghy half-filled up with icy brine, and we caught
nothing but a single eel, which I remember hacking then
to death as a goddamned makeshift offering, the sea
at last relented to leave us on the dusty farther shore.

•

As for Burnsey, I hope he stayed afloat awhile before
the sea pulled him finally under. Afterwards, we paid
the boatman what we owed, then strolled back down
to Bob's, boasting of our brush with death, and of just
how brave we'd been, then turned the talk to supper, and of
the night that lie ahead, and would the local girls be there.

THE SWEATER

Loomed my first real Saturday night date.
My father winked and beamed as he led me
into the master bedroom, where he unstuck
the bottom drawer of his highboy dresser
so he might bestow on his firstborn, & newest buck

on the block—about to be initiated into the mysterious,
Eleusynian, head-spinning, perfumed world
of women (and who knew what other ecstasies)—
his Sunday best & dashing cashmere sweater.
I watched his dark eyes blaze with memories

of his own lost mythic youth even as he spoke.
This was almost fifty years ago, so that he still
had half a foot and fifty pounds on me. But if
I flexed both my so-called biceps, and kept
my narrow shoulders, rigor mortis military stiff,

and if I sucked in air in some sort of blowfish
style I might—just might—make his sweater fit.
Ah, this was it, he whistled: my first bestowment,
bar mitzvah, confirmation, manhood's
yummy threshold & inner sanctum moment.

I was just sixteen, and so (alas) would need
to take three emasculating buses OR be driven
by my father in the family's green two-toned
'47 Pontiac to the other side of town
to retrieve my beautiful blue-eyed blond.

Ah, she, with her Cinderella curls and crinkled smile,
God's own sweet angel bathed in an unearthly light
who had somehow (inexplicably) said yes (yes!)
when I'd asked her out to see Charlton (Moses)
Heston take out Pharaoh's boys & all his armored horses.

Alas, came my father's sage advice along with his
borrowed sweater. *Shake the father's hand,* he boomed.
*Be firm, but don't try to grind his knuckles. Sweet talk
the mother, yes her this, her that. Oh, and as for
the girl, laugh at all her silly little jokes, walk*

*on the outside, play the gentleman, & don't ever let her
catch you staring down her blouse. Most of all, my boy,
take extra special care with that cashmere sweater.*
Mother, who'd heard it all before, groaned at the bull,
such as she'd suffered all these years Mr. Wonderful

had been dishing out so lavishly, and had her own advice
to offer now. *Treat the girl the way you'd treat your mother
or your sister's friends. Be polite, laugh, have fun,
and remember how lucky any girl would be to be
going out with her sweet, smart, oh-so-handsome son.*

Thus, decked out in my father's too-huge sweater,
the looming night advanced as looming nights will do.
And yet a sweet time, too, it was, and lyrical and poignant.
And very nearly a success. Except that, by the time
we left Moses back there at the movie, the Fates had sent

25

the Red Sea conspiring up our way, backing up along
the gutters & the sidewalks while we waited on the corner
for my gallant father, who showed up hours late
to chauffeur me & my half-drowned Cinderella home.
And that was that. Except what I learned about the fate

of sons who willy-nilly step too soon into their father's
place and so must pay the price. And though I never
dated her again, I hope she's blessed as I have been and—better—
doles out wisdom to her kids sounder than I got when I handed
back my father his ruined (imitation) cashmere sweater.

WORK

And so it went, day after day, the four of us, inching
out from the shallow end of the empty Empire
Swimming Pool, the ritual of gearing up to sandblast,
preparing to engorge our peck's worth of aqua
metal dust. Worse was the glare off the rain-scum slop
congealing at the deeper end, the sun's reflection
blinding us whenever we looked back. In silence
I pushed on beneath the blazing sun, without benefit
of radio or the consolations of Bo Diddley
and the King to ease me through my hell.

On my left, with a caged panther's padfoot instinct
stalked my father, gray threading at forty
his samite-sheeted hair, his jaws working as he plotted
how to keep a wife and six kids fed, bent on getting
a day's work out of each of us even if it killed him,
and the bitching sun didn't beat him to the punch.
By half past nine of the sixth day it was making
good on that promise as we brushed the pool
a coat of ether-blistering blue. Robin's egg blue,
Florida blue, Blue Pompeian, Bay of Naples Blue,
Côte d'Azur, Disney blue, the veriest blue of blue,
that would transform fifteen thousand gallons of chlorine
threaded water which my father would at last unleash
like some second Moses, so that seven hundred day camp
kids might splash about, fluttering their flashing feet,
squealing the squeals of a too too happy summer.

That epiphany still stood two weeks off. Meanwhile
there were cabins to Lysol-rinse, a pony and two
palominos to quarter (illegally) on the abutting
state preserve, and Rusty the Little Choo-Choo
to set chugging once again along the western
chainlink fence patrolled each dusk by the boss's
two German Shepherds. Come September, I would hie
me off to the fall-gold hills of Beacon Prep, where I
would rise at six each morning to chant antiphonally
a version of the Office, then struggle with fourth-year
Latin, singing of the epic birth of that other empire
forming on the sunken Tiber's sullen banks.

But for now that kingdom of the mind lay starboard
off, an oasis only, beckoning. Here, inside this
blazing pit ruled silence, punctuated by the bark
of orders from a man who had a pool to finish,
brushstroke by numbing brushstroke, blood-thick paint
baking the metal and our hands under an Egyptian sun,
while darkened each day more my princely skin
that now began to peel away like antique mottled
rolls of stippled wallpaper. *Sunt lacrimae rerum*.
Prisons are a state of mind. Oases ditto. Somewhere,
I'd heard, were words and plashing water. A lake, a rope,
a lifting up, a letting go. Somewhere too applause, a plunge
down deepward, and bubbles rising slowly to the top.

The Place across the River

Often I think of them, their shadows filing
through the fall's first snowfall out
toward the lower playing fields. Of
O'Brien hunched against the cold in his green
Deerfield parka there on the sidelines,

soft words steadying the novice quarterback
sacked in the first minute of the game.
Of Melvoin pointing toward the laminated
map of Asia, 8:15 of a Monday morning,
prodding his perplexed & somnolent students—

among whom no doubt slouched some of tomorrow's
earthshakers—into at least considering the moral
fallout of the Bomb. Or the headmaster's face,
lighting up as the stammering ninth grader
began unpacking some algebraic theorem. Fraker,

staring out the window towards the budding
maples along the river, through which Mohawk
& Iroquois once fanned towards the embattled
settlement, wondering how this boy or that
was faring now in the vast cold world that lies

beyond the purple-umber hills to east and west.
Signor Garcia, who left behind a law office
in old Havana so that he might discourse here
in New England on the past perfect of the verb *estar*
to fifteen-year-olds from Akron & Toledo.

I think too of the Zen-like Mr. Young,
of that Falstaffian grin of Hodermarsky's,
who painted landscapes one might believe in,
and of genial Jim Smith, who taught his boys
there was a more to playing than the final tally,

and almost made the boys believe it too.
And the others, too: Littwin, Tyler, Henry,
Hemingway & those whose names I cannot
now remember, some of whom lie under
the earth's lid, who once took boys from Cicero,

Four Corners, Beirut and the Bronx,
year after year, my three double day-go
sons among them, just as they were,
Boston bankers' well-heeled sons & the sons
of Brooklyn teamsters, molding each

as each would let himself be molded.
Mornings, until they learned to drive themselves,
I packed my sons into the clunking orange Pinto,
prepared to hand them over to the care of men
like these, understanding only dimly then that I was

asking them to take each buzzing mass
of needs, among so many others, and somehow
turn them into gentlemen with hawk-bright eyes
and quips for each occasion and a hatred
of injustice. Which, as one thinks back on it,

meant asking for nothing short of the miraculous
from a company of men who believed in what
they did & did it, rising from their allotted
places in the crowded dining hall each morning
early, ready to begin another blessèd day.

THE THINGS THEY TAUGHT ME

i

Except on green imitation leather rosters
long since gone to yellow, or asleep now
somewhere in the vaults of Whitmore Hall,
most of their names are lost to me,
covered palimpsest-wise by others
coming after, each class growing
outward like rings about some
blasted tree of knowledge which
somehow sends forth its yearly
shoots, though I can still make out
many of those vivid quizzing faces
by the peach-blush light of memory.

ii

From that November afternoon back
at Colgate thirty years ago, a neophyte
patting himself on the back for teaching
so crisply & deliciously on death
& dying in the work of Hemingway,
then suddenly hearing the news from the car
radio outside the great gray shale-stone building
that the president had been shot in Dallas,
I understood there were lessons
to be learned, even on bucolic granite
leaf-strewn quadrangles, and that I was
just then being taught a hard one.

Or on this campus back in the spring
of '70, I lost myself—*nel mezzo del
cammin*—in the middle of a nightmare
as the endless war began spilling over into
other countries. Young men like those
I'd taught were going under by the thousands
in leech-thick paddies, while a mad karma roiled
back on us at home. Dazed prophets
stoned on LSD & armed with bullhorns
began patrolling administration centers
that seemed to hunker down like toad
presidios. By the flare of the brave
new order one watched ghost trundles
begin rumbling across each campus.
No one over thirty could be trusted.
A girl of nineteen, flowers braiding
her fairy waistlong hair, played
a novice campus cop. "Come on,"
she kept coaxing, "let me have your
gun. That way no one will be hurt."
In the lotus-fevered milling dark
I watched unbelieving as she offered
him a ring of broken daisies.

With teaching halted, there were
those who came Nicodemus-like by night
to see me. They didn't give a damn
about a grade, I was to understand, not
while this dirty little war was going on.
Unless of course the grade could be
hitched up to a B or better. Insurance,
I was made to understand, in case
the Mother of all Revolutions fizzled.

iii
That was the one side. To learn
they were only like the rest of us:
innocent, filled with their own delusions,
less than perfect. The other side
was knowledge stored, a honeyed
wisdom gathered drop by drop.
From bouncing biases & gaucheries
off so many captive ears, I finally came to
understand that each voice out there
in the classroom might in a single brilliant
instant reveal yet one more spoke of the great
& fiery wheel the prophets sing of.

How often too their words, reshaped
& polished, like the refurbished Hubbell
Scope, opened up on galaxies of thought
I had not known till then existed.
In the give and take of the strobic
Time-lapsed dance before the blackboard,
one comes to taste at last the Spirit's
gifts: wisdom, insight, reverence, patience,
heart, the knowing when to speak & when
to hold one's fire. Otherwise what one
does up there before the class becomes
mere peacock strut, the dazzling wit
which fears all difference, the small
self-interests of the tenured jackal.

iv

"If they hadn't paid me to come
and teach," the poet Randall Jarrell
once wrote, "I'd have gladly paid
to have the privilege." My sentiments
exactly, though bread being what it is,
& rent, & books, and having pored now
over ten thousand thousand papers—towers
of ivory, yes, though there were (in truth)
whole ziggurats of psychobabble too—
I'm relieved to see it work the way it has:
this being paid for what one loves to do.

"Still, you won't know until the best
of it is over what the real gifts were,"
Levine told me years ago, another teacher/
poet who'd seen forty years of it
in classrooms much like these,
glare-lit, off-white waiting rooms
one finds in registries & morgues.
He was right, for the real payoff, once
I was smart enough to see, was what
my students taught me, though I never
told them, the story being that it was
I who'd been sent to do the teaching.

Induction, The University of Massachusetts,
Massachusetts Nu Chapter, Phi Beta Kappa,
 25 May 1996.

Failed Ghazal against the Siren Call of morpheus & In Niggling Praise of Old Bitch Fame, Rejected (Gently) by the Late Agha Shahid Ali

Soft down pillow, quilts, post-prandial naps. No, kid, that's not how
One wins one's bays. Sloth. Hell, Dante knew that trap. That's not how

One's name buys those extra twenty years most of us can hope for.
Take Hyakutaki, our latest cosmic flap. No, that's not how

You do it, one brief return engagement every 15,000 years.
Forget the papers & all the starstruck crap. That's not how

You make your mark in this vast & yawning universe, mit naps.
Stay awake. Hot coffee, the self-inflicted slap. Not under quilts is how

You win crisp laurels. When your breathing stops then sleep, not now.
Nix that morphic nap. You listening? A snooze, a girl, & ices is not how.

UNSOLICITED

In memoriam all editors of poetry mags, anthologies, contests, etc.

Poem after poem keeps tumbling in,
Most computer-spawned, and in different fonts.
A few typed onionskin, the odd one
Scrawled in pencil, erased, redone. One wants

To respond, if not in kind, then—better—
Kindly, to each and every poem: the earnest ones,
The ones accompanied with the proper letter
Like a doting mother, the witty ones (with puns),

The ten-page epic, the tanka & the haiku (lopped),
The yellowed odes to butterflies & sad elm trees,
The mythy sequence on awkward stilts that flopped,
The embalmed canary elegy, decked out with fleas.

And on it goes, in spite of the tired saw that goes
There are more poets out there, friend, than readers for
The goddamn poems themselves. Which means, God knows,
We all want some one to hear us above the aphasic roar

And stop a moment and turn and tell us, yes, they've heard.
They've heard, and more, acknowledge what we've said.
And that it matters (what we've said) and, yes, in this absurd
World where so little matters, the soul is (for an instant) fed.

And so, day by day the poems go on getting written, then mailed
To, yes, yours truly, with such high hopes in every one
It hurts to stamp them failed & failed & failed
For the odd one among the rest that sings, Ain't we got fun.

ABSENCE OF CROCUS

Eleven days till spring. Two hundred
sixty-four hours, sixteen minutes.
That's how one counts the coming on
of spring here in New England.
Eleven days, more or less. Less
or more. The thermometer outside
my kitchen window sticks at ten
below. Chilling news to say
that, if the sky is blue, it is the blue
of an S.S. Überkommander's eyes,
a blue made bluer by two
feet of snow spinning crabwise
down for the past three days, my
unoffending chest screaming
with the pain of digging trenches
from the back porch to the Ford
buried somewhere out there
beneath all that anti-manna manna.

What shall I make of a much diminished
thing, of two pale crocuses fronting
the western wind. *There must be*
in all of this a lesson, said the preacher,
after his rambling sermon. *But I'll be*
damned if I know what it is. O blessèd
saint of similes and metaphors, whoever
you may be, help me out this once.

You see these crocuses I have labored
over all these years. Make them please

cohere. Let them flourish as you did
with Dante into some grand flowering
symbol. Two crocuses heralding
the coming on of spring, pale purple things,
fronting the bitter cold. Like those
Bowmen of Shu, stiff in their frozen trenches
facing the Northern foe, as they dreamt on
of those citron cities to the south.

LIGHT

Strange how it strikes you, that special light.
An old light, really, if light is ever old,
a light memory has kindled this afternoon. Or
is it the light that kindles memory instead,
flooding in so quietly you start from your
reverie to follow where it leads? A light.

A peculiar and special light. Let's say the light
of some special place. Let's say a Vermont mountain
light, brightening an inn and cottages, green shade
heightening the bright impasto-yellow fountain-
falling light of late August. A light made
as if for this one place alone, a late summer's light

illuminating a glass pitcher on an old oak
dresser, while the laughter of those gathered runs on
across the field, rippling outward before it disappears.
Light on a pitcher in a Shaker-simple room, alone.
How is it this image only lingers after all these years?
Fifteen summers, gone, gone at a single stroke.

And so many I loved gone with them. Sad-eyed Terrence gone
And—ah!—Gardner gone and Nemerov. And Wild Bill gone,
gone across the Styx, ferried to the other shore.
And others gone, whose names I have forgotten,
some gesture all that's left of all that went before,
crystal shattered in some smalltime palace revolution.

Gone too, though still this side of Stygia, Phil, and Don,
who used to sketch out in the lower hay-mown field.
And Wyatt gone, with whom I walked those roads,
and Mark and David gone, and Bob, who would not yield
to time or pressure or those petty academic toads. . . .
Gone, gone away, all the brilliant ones long gone.

Yes, Linda gone, and Nancy. My lovely ones all gone,
long packed and gone, their shades still hovering
on those old laugh-haunted porches like fireflies
on summer nights. Gone all of it, evening covering
all but the memory, where now a light alone abides,
gilding a pitcher and the dresser it has settled on.

TWO

CASUALTY REPORT

The car coming on, then crossing the divide,
you at the wheel, distracted by our earlier fight.
Blood on the dash, blood on the steering wheel, your
sweet face shattered in an instant, so that the slant light

still, after fifteen years, reveals the seismographic scar
across your upper lip. Harm done to others, harm
to myself. After all these years my words, however
well-intentioned, fail like the useless charm

words so often are. Too many nights you've heard me start
from some fitful, endragoned sleep, thrashing in the chill
eddying of first dawn, my heart thumping
against its savage cage of bone, replaying still

the oncoming car, swerving, then crossing the divide.
How many times I've startled into night,
relieved to find you sleeping there beside me,
like some brave new world in the uncertain light

off starboard, a gift of such proportions it still
amazes. Live long enough, and we will surely all
turn up on someone's list: the accident report
filed by the trooper at the scene, the hospital

bed with its checklist, where this time it's you awake
all night, and me an obit in the morning paper. And there
you have it, the latest casualty noted over coffee,
before I rise up at last to rinse the silverware

in the kitchen sink, replaying the morning's latest
tragedy over in my mind, the way I've done so
many times before, wondering if I just might get
the right words said this time, or simply let it go.

FEAR

For Bill Matthews (1943–1998)

He looked down at his desk to find it waiting there.
Fear. Blank fear emanating from the face there
on the page, as so often fear had stalked him
in the reaches of the night. True, the face was smiling.
And yet it seemed to darken the room around it.
Outside the bleak trees stood: wordless, bare, unlit.

A busy day inside. Work mounting up, small
kudos from an editor, a stubborn paragraph
reshaped to both their satisfactions, two essays read,
a letter sent, three bills paid, a student with a lame
excuse off the hook because of his largesse.
Of this and this we measure our success.

Or so he had believed. But now the gray face
of his friend kept staring up at him. A friend just younger
than himself, who now would always stay that way.
A friend he liked to think of as living on some
Tuscan mountain farm, like Horace, the acid wit half-hid
by the Wild Bill mustache and the drooping lid.

For a time his friend had sung like no one else
and his friend had made him laugh.
And now his friend was dead. And if the truth
be told, his friend had written so damned well
he'd come to fear him, each squeezed-off shot a hit,
neither short nor wide. How had he done it?

Still, he counted him his friend, one who could quaff
age-old Falernian with Mingus, Martial, Bird.
Once, seated at the opera, his friend had kissed
his fingers to the staccato flight of some stout soprano
basting slowly in her painted armor. Each had shown
him how to wring a music he could call his own,

and in time the man had made himself that music. And now,
too soon, the man alas was gone. The trees stood
naked in the autumn air. The gray face only seemed
to wink at him. So there it was: his friend become
at last a book. Somewhere a fat lady began with dread
to sweat a gorgeous aria. His friend was dead.

SILT

How it steals up on you, this mortality,
dropping its calling card, say, after the flight
back from your friend's wedding. Six kinds of wine
on a stone veranda overlooking the starlit sea,

while migrants labored in the fields beneath.
One morning you bend down to lace
your sneakers and find your leg stiff as a base-
ball bat. How many times you told yourself Death

wouldn't catch you unaware, the way, alas,
it did so many of your friends. That you'd hie
yourself off to the hospital at the first sign
of trouble. And then, when it should happen, as

it has, you go into denial once again, while your
sad leg whimpers for attention, until at last you get
the doctor, who finds a fourteen-inch blood clot
silting up your veins there on the sonar.

Mortality's the sticking thinners twice
each day into your stomach, until the skin screams
a preternatural black and blue. Mortality's
swallowing the stuff they use to hemorrhage mice.

It's botched blood tests for months on end.
Admit it, what's more boring than listening to
another's troubles, except thumbing through
postcards of others on vacation. Friendly Finland,

Warsaw in July. Mortality's my leg, her arm, your heart.
Besides, who gives a damn about the plight of others,
except the saints and God? But isn't death the mother
of us all? Shouldn't death mean caring, the moving out

at last beyond the narrow self? But who has
time for that? Six wines on a stone veranda,
stars, a summer moon high over Santa Monica,
cigars from verboten old Havana, live jazz.

That's what one wants. That, and not some blood
clot clogging up one's veins. No poet will ever
touch again what Dante somehow touched there
at the *Paradiso*'s end. It was there he had St. Bernard

beseech his Lady to look upon him that she might
grant him light and understanding, which he might
share in turn with others. Lady, cast thine eyes,
I pray thee, down toward me. I cannot take much height,

though God knows I've tried. Six wines, two cigars,
a summer moon over the veranda, where I kept tilting
outwards, my veins absorbing even then the *gravitas* of silting,
while Love was busy moving the sun and other stars.

Pietà

New Year's Eve, a party at my brother's.
Hats, favors, the whole shebang, as we waited
for one world to die into another.

And still it took three martinis before
she could bring herself to say it. How
the body of her grown son lay alone there

in the ward, just skin & bone, the nurses
masked & huddled in the doorway, afraid
to cross over into a world no one seemed

to understand. This was a dozen years ago,
you have to understand, before the thing
her boy had had become a household word.

Consider Martha. Consider Lazarus four days gone.
If only you'd been here, she says, *if only
you'd been here*. And no one now to comfort her,

no one except this priest, she says, an old
friend who'd stood beside them through the dark
night of it all, a bull-like man, skin black

as the black he wore, the only one who seemed
willing to walk across death's threshold into
that room. And now, she says, when the death

was over, to see him lift her son, light as a baby
with the changes death had wrought, and cradle him
like that, then sing him on his way, a cross

between a lullaby & blues, *mmm hmmm*, while
the nurses, still not understanding what they saw,
stayed outside and watched them from the door.

Passage

So I opened the little book she'd placed
there on the table and half-shouted since
she didn't have her hearing aids plugged in,
and read aloud the passage she'd pointed to:
the one about prayer sometimes being all
one has to link you to your loved ones,
especially where death or distance have
come between. She turned to her husband
of sixty years, still working over his bowl
of branflakes. *Did you hear that*, Phil,
she said, to which my father-in-law,
half-startled, bobbed his head, yes, yes,
though probably he hadn't. Then she turned
to me, eyes burning with the bituminous
shine of a girl of twenty.
                    I have known
this woman now for forty years,
yet never once saw her search my face
like this, with the beseeching gaze of
a baby robin waiting to be fed. Besides,
she was fast approaching the threshold
now of some great mystery. She wanted
to be fed and I had fed her as
I could, with the words I witnessed
turn to bread before us on the table.

EXILE
Magnificat anima mea . . .

Hands folded over the child she bears,
as if in prayer, as if protecting him, she moves
across this abstract plane as did her forebears,
who once fled out of Egypt. Her eyes: half-intent

on the fiery pillar that mushrooms up before, half
on something it is not given us to see. Black
the canvas, night pregnant with a million stars,
earl stars, fireflakes struck off Dante's blazing brand.

And are those stones her bare feet sweep across?
Or bleached skulls, recalling the million million dead
in the killing fields and camps? The dead in Bethlehem,
the dead at Calvary, her son among them. The millions

of pilgrims down the ages, all in flight from or flight toward.
And this woman, heavy with solitude and child, heavy with
sorrow but with promise too, her baby magnified with each passing
heartbeat, cell by cell by cell, as we ourselves are magnified in turn.

MOTHER OF CONSOLATION

What you look hard at looks back hard at you.
As in this icon, where the child with the deer-
brown eyes gazes at something just beyond
your view: this infant king blessing everywhere.

Blood of her blood, bone of her bone.
Identical the mouth, the nose, the eyes.
You can see he is his mother's son, and hers alone,
in any way one's DNA supplies.

If too he is his Father's Son, how can you know
but by the blazing love behind the gaze, or in
the innocence of blessing? Even then there's no
way to know until you touch the mystery within.

And as for that, you will have first to understand
what it is you gaze on with the same dim eyes
that have too long settled on the sensual, the bland,
the million sighing flyspecked buzzing lies.

The scrim of sight is dimmed with sick desire.
The Buddha knew this, and Blake, and Dante too.
How hard, how hard it is to re-ignite the fire,
the inner flame that lets you look upon these two,

these two whose gaze gives back such peace again,
but only if you learn to turn the outward gaze inward to
the gaze within, the child's eyes remembering the When,
and the mother's doe-brown eyes gazing back at you.

WOLF MOON

My father, two months shy now of his eighty-fifth,
lies weighted down by two blown knees, edema,
arthritis, loss of hearing, emphysema,
reduced to wearing sweatpants underneath his shift

to keep some shred of dignity in a provincial hospital
four hundred miles south of where I live. Groan
after garbled groan spills over into my telephone,
mixed with clumps of undigested syllables.

Meanwhile, my bewildered wife has gone to stay
with her aged father, diagnosed with cancer of the lung,
while her mild mother lully lully drifts among
the stars, before she settles back into her bed in Rockaway.

Wolf moon, wolf moon, prowling the evening sky,
as you have these sixty Januaries past
above abandoned rooms where I have passed
those selfsame years (and some), explain once more why

what happens has to happen. Tell me, ancient moon, why
the old keep trudging up the line, dazed with fear.
Send my way, sir, some drugged truth I can bear,
as now the old ones fall away and we limp up to die.

FERRY CROSSING

Beyond the granite breakers, a world of roiling
waters & raging spume & graygreen troughing
waves. Gulls hovering in the downdraft of a boiling
wake. Beneath it all, beneath the thrum of chuffing

engines, the endless wailing voices. Three days with my father, old
now, pointing out the same unvarying scenes once more
as I drove his car: those conning towers staring still into the cold
Atlantic, while the waves grind against the battered shore.

Three days. Then, his morning, north to Lewes and Cape May.
Late March, and daffodils unfurling, and snow-white
blossoms on the trembling branch, and spring still hard at bay.
And now the ferry wheezing to keep the further shore in sight.

All my life the chitter of the living has mixed together with the dead.
As now, faintly audible beneath the TV racket and video arcades—
that white cascade of noise by which our daily world is fed—
the charged static of the lost crackling as the world about me fades.

No doubt they want to tell me something they think I need
to hear, but try as I may, I cannot make what they're saying out.
Something about life, no doubt. Or about the end of life, a river feed-
ing the endless ocean, as if they knew what death was all about. . . .

You'd think my father, at eighty-five, would know more
about the final things. But if he does he isn't telling me.
Instead, he'd rather suck the last drop from the rind, poor,
dear man, in spite of his shallow breathing, bad hip, arthritic knee.

And who can blame him? All his brothers & sisters have now crossed
over to the other shore, and both his wives as well. What looms
large for him these days is the Silverado hubcap he says he lost
when the curb attacked his '87 Caddy, and which accouterment he assumes

(rightly) I will replace for him, since it has become the whirling
epicenter of his shrinking world. The Caddy has by now become his wife,
yearning each Sunday for some final spin. Meanwhile the waves keep hurling
against the prow, as we hold on for life. This mindless, precious life.

Fathers & Sons

The boy sits on the edge of the iron bed, both
feet inches off the floor, rocking back & forth,
forth & back, clutching the brown paper bag
containing his clean socks & his hairbrush,
as he watches the slant tick tock of sunlight
inch over the floorboards, the blue shadows
growing longer & longer as they darken the twin

rows of beds, and the streetlights come on.
Like the wise virgin in the story, he keeps watch
for his father, while the nice woman smiles her smile,
leaving, then coming back, leaving, and back, trying
to coax him out of the coat he's buttoned to his neck.
Out in the yard, his close-cropped small brother stalks
the iron-spiked fence, back & forth, forth & back,

once running after a man on the outside he shouts
is his father, but isn't. In the dark interstices
of the late autumn evening, defeated at last, when
their lamps have gone out & still the king fails
to appear, the boy on the bed is led down to his brother
& the other lost boys in the dining room hall
for turkey & turnips & to sing praise to their God.

Fast forward fifty Thanksgivings and here
they are again: the once-divorced, twice-widowed
father with his two graying sons, along with their wives
& grown children and one babbling grandbaby
there at the table, and three kinds of wine & a meal,
as he liked to say, fit for a king. A lost king who came
years late for his kids, & swept them up in his Ford

& waved adieu to the redbrick orphanage, and bought
them ice cream in the drugstore by the bridge (any flavor
they wanted), but never explained, then or thereafter,
what kept him from coming to get them, and who can't
for the love of him remember now what happened,
or why one son seems to see right through him
and why the other can't seem to see him right enough.

Death of the Father

My son, take care of your father when he is old;
grieve him not as long as he lives.
Even if his mind fail, be considerate of him. . . .

The Book of Sirach

Tide out, & the long hall empty & the silent room,
the crumpled form who was my father hooked up
to the oxygen, morphine-drowned, the crucifix
floating above his fevered bed, the labored
breathing growing shallower by the minute.

This is the hand, the right hand, mottled black
and blue now with a hundred intravenous needles,
the hand that held me as a child and fed me,
the grimegrained fist that held the ballpeen hammer
and the massive wrench, and smashed my face

when I was young and bold, and that I sang of once
in lines of stunned, astonished, underwater rage & sorrow
with this my own right hand some twenty years ago.
Done—fiat—at the Sabbath table, my siblings
and my dear dead mother bobbing there as seawracked

witnesses in a grainy nightmare replayed a thousand times
since then, one from which I never did escape. And now
my time alone here with my father nearly up. When he starts
from sleep it is only for a moment, and then to fix an eye
on the stranded figure of his oldest son afloat before him.

What we had time to say in the forty years between
the oceanic then and now we have either said or kept
ourselves from saying, or said only with our eyes to read
as best they could. Day in, day out, month after month,
I tended to his needs, gave comfort, and—if the truth

be told—received it in return, and laughter too. Once—
relieved to see me when the nurses circled round—
he grabbed my hand and kissed it. Fourteen months,
fourteen exhausting months of it: the wheelchair strolls
down these same prison corridors, the spinach down

his bib, the stories misremembered. And now, on this
late summer's night, his last, a pale yellow light floating
from the nurses' station and reflected off the crossbar
above his head, the room is dark, dark & dark, so that
I must grope now for his hand, his right hand, the one,

wondering what the years between—had he had money
& mildness enough—might otherwise have held, years
when time itself seemed long & endless, and fold it in my own—
helpless as he is, and kiss it, blessing him for all he did or meant
to do before the darkness takes him away for good.

How It All Worked Out

Come, sighed the Voices. *This way. Now. It's late.*
The crowd, upon inspection, seemed ready too. Shook
then that wide stadium with shouts. Dignitaries in black
began the long procession toward the ivory gate.

My shroud (a single piece of linen, with matching hood)
seemed outré, yet absolutely right for whatever
august event should now reveal itself. How clever,
I remember thinking then, that the voices out there should

be shouting in a tongue I seemed to but could not
understand. *Come*, they summoned yet again. *Isn't this
what you spent your life preparing for? Artful death? Wish
then for this. But whether you choose the Thing itself or not,*

ready must you be. And here it is. I would have fled
then, you understand, as every blood cell cried
out for me to do. But all self-will had died.
Surely, I warmed myself, *it will be better for me dead,*

or what's a heaven for? An ill-lit passage led
up a dripping ramp. Smoking torches and dried
blood lined the ancient granite walls. I tried
to keep my mind on something as I trudged ahead.

What was waiting out there by the ivory gate? Were they
friend or foe shouting for us up there in the stands?
A milky light beckoned as the line moved up. Bands
blended—drums, flute, winds—in the uplift of some way-

ward breeze. *So here it finally is*, I remember
memory remembering then, there on the threshold & could hear
the wind howling down the empty passage of my one good ear.
Then total silence and a blinding light. As I remember.

SHADOW OF THE FATHER

How shall I approach you, Joseph, you, the shadow
   of the Father? The stories vary. But who
      were you really? Were you young? Old?

A widower, with children of your own, as the *Proto-*
   evangelium says? I have been to bloody Bethlehem
      and seen the orphaned children there.

A small town, where Palestinian gunmen roamed the Church
   of the Nativity, while Israeli snipers watched
      from the adjoining rooftops. It is a scene not all that

different from Herod's horsemen hunting down a baby,
   though you, dreamer that you were, had already heeded
      the midnight warning and fled with Mary and the baby.

And though they failed to find him, you found him, Joseph,
   and raised him, teaching him your trade, two day laborers
      who must often have queued up, looking for work.

How difficult it must have been, standing in, as every father
   must sometimes feel. Yet where else did your son find
      his courage and outrage against injustice?

How did he become the man he was, if not for you? *"Didn't you know*
I had to be about my father's business?" Thus the boy, at twelve,
there in Jerusalem. Words which must have wounded,

though they put the matter in its proper light. After that, you drop
from history. Saint of happy deaths, was yours a happy death?
Tradition says it was, logic seems to say it was,

with that good woman and that sweet son there by your side. For the past
two months my wife and her sister have been caring for their
father, who is dying of cancer. There is the hospital bed,

the potty, the rows of medicine to ease the growing pain. From time
to time he starts up from his recliner to count his daughters
and his agèd Irish bride, thinking of a future he no longer

has. When she was little, my wife once told me, she prayed daily
in the church of St. Benedict to you that she might
have a daily missal. One day, a man in coveralls

came up to her and—without a word—gave her one with your name
on it. Oh, she said, her parents would never allow it.
Put a penny in the poor box, he smiled,

then turned, and disappeared forever. *Who was he?* I asked.
   You know as well as I do who he was, was all she'd say.
      Joseph, be with her now, and with her father, as he faces

the great mystery, as we all must at the end, alone. You seem
   like so many other fathers, who have watched over
      their families, not knowing what the right words were,

but willing to be there for them, up to the very end. Be with them now,
   as you have been for so many others. Give them strength.
      And come, if need be, in a dream, as the angel came to you,

and came to that other Joseph in Egypt so many years before. Be there,
   as once you were in Bethlehem and Nazareth and Queens.
      You, good man, dreamer, the shadow of the Father.

THREE

P.S.

But is it true to say, "better the past as book,
the story sipped in small and smaller doses,
then left off mid-sentence by the night lamp,
the final page left off in half-legible italics"?
Nine out of ten seem resigned to have it so.
There's Señor X and Madame Y, three rows back,
nodding their assent. Friend Horace ditto.
The past revisited without the noise or smell.
The way memory says it was. But revamped
now. Lavendered. With a minim dose of pain.

Or this: life surging at the end like wires crossed.
Roses, after all this time, come round again as roses.
Dry straw green again, last year's shoots unfurling, damp.
Death knolls, tolling backwards, sounding the wedding bell.
Sodden embers by the sudden great wind tossed
high and higher, winnowed into virgin flame again.

Making Capital

*I cannot in conscience spend time on poetry, neither have I the inducements
and inspirations that make others compose. Feeling, love in particular, is the
great moving power and spring of verse and the only person that I am in
love with seldom, especially now, stirs my heart sensibly and when he does I
cannot always 'make capital' of it, it would be a sacrilege to do so. Then
again I have of myself made verse so laborious.*

    Gerard Manley Hopkins to Robert Bridges, 15 February 1879

For six weeks I've tried lassoing the wind
and come up with nada, zip & zero. Oh, I *know*
what moved me then, what sweet whisperings to the mind,
but could not make those protean shapes sit still, though

God knows I've tried. Sunday Mass. The eight.
My wife there next to me, thinking her own deep
thoughts. Congealed light on the pews, cold as Fate,
candles guttering, half the parishioners half asleep.

And the priest up at the pulpit, embellishing a story taken
from one of those Chicken Soup series for the soul.
I kept glancing left, then down, then right. Forsaken
the place, as if the Good News had dropped down some black hole,

paralyzed by what the papers had been screaming now
of scandal, indifferent to whatever the poor priest had to say.
Then, suddenly, up there at the altar, I caught a shadow
stirring, as if struggling up the hill under the heaving sway

of thornwood. Young Isaac, carrying kindling for a fire,
branches his shaken father had ordered him to fetch.
The figure trembled in the ether, then gave way to yet another,
whose wrists they'd roped to a wooden crossbeam (poor wretch),

as he too stumbled toward the distant rise. But what
had this to do with where I found myself? Everything,
I guess. Or nothing. Depending on the view. True, the rot
of the beholder went deep, deep, but deeper went the blessing:

the thought that God had spared the first from death, but not
the other, who among the trees had begged his father not to drink
the cup. All that history in a blink, as the one went on to populate
a nation, while the other—nailed to that wood—rose from the stink

of death, promising to lift us with him. I looked around
the church, knowing what I know of death: the death of mother,
father, friends, the death of promise, of vision run aground,
death of self, of all we might have been, death of that ideal other,

the bitter end of all. Nada, zip . . . Except for that loop in time, when
something gave: a blip of light across the mind's dark eye, if you
can call it that. But what, if not a good man going under? Then
struggling to raise himself again, bent on doing what he had to do.

DEATH & TRANSFIGURATION

Down the precipitous switchbacks at eighty
the pokerfaced Palestinian cabby aims his Mercedes
while the three of us, ersatz pilgrims, blank-eyed, lurch,
and the droll Franciscan goes on about the Art Deco Church

of the Transfiguration crowning the summit of the Mount.
Up there I'd touched the damp stones of the old Crusader fount,
paced the thick walls, imagined Muslims circling below
on horseback, muleback, then ascending for the final blow.

A decent pasta and a dry wine, thanks to the Fratelli who run
the hostel at the site, followed by an even drier lecture in the sun-
drenched court, then back down to the glinting taxis, ready
to return us now to the same old, feverish, unsteady

world half a mile below. I thought of the old masters, so
many of them who had tried to ignite this scene: Angelico,
di Buoninsegna, Bellini, Perugino, the Frenchman John of Berry,
the Preobrazheniye (Russian, Novgorod, sixteenth century),

and thought at last of what Raphael had wrought. It was to be
his final work, commissioned for some French cathedral, his early
death at thirty-seven intervening. For those who only dream
of some vertiginous, longed-for transfiguration, he would seem

to hold out something magnanimous and large: the benzine brightness
of the Christ, eyes upraised in the atom flash of whiteness,
that body lifted up, cloud-suspended feet above the earth. There,
on either side, with the Tablets and the Book: Moses and Elijah.

74

Below, his fear-bedazzled friends: Peter, James, and John. And though
paint is only paint, we can almost hear the Father's words again, so
caught up in the vision was the artist: *This is my beloved Son,*
on whom my favor rests. Listen to him. Meanwhile, someone

in the lower half of the picture is gesturing toward the transfigured
Christ. He is part of the curious and anxious crowd
that surrounds the epileptic youth, whose eyes, like Christ's, are wide,
but wide with seizure like some frenzied Sibyl's: the great divide

that separates him from the others, as if he understood the same strange
thing Raphael came to see as he composed this scene: that the deranged
youth has somehow come upon a mystery. Like us, he has been bound
round with fear, and only the One descending as he comes can sound

those depths of cosmic light and dark, in which the young man
writhes honeystuck in death, though he will—the gospel says—be raised again
to health and to his father, in this prologue to the resurrection.
That's it, then, it would seem: first the old fears descending, then dejection

and the dunning sameness in the daily going round and round of things.
Then a light like ten thousand suns that flames the brain and brings
another kind of death with it, and then—once more—the daily round
again. But changed now by what the blind beseeching eye has found.

NINE ONE ONE

Once again the nightmare. The blueblack plume,
The billowing flame. All my life I've been afraid
Of tall buildings, and here was the tallest, down
At Manhattan's prow. Firemen and police officers
Kept running *toward* the flames! People were falling
Or jumping. No one yet seemed to understand
What was happening. How will they put it out,
I kept wondering. Then the second tower.
Then the Pentagon. Then a fourth jet, down

Somewhere over Pennsylvania. Reality itself
Seemed to buckle with the buckling towers.
"Mourn for the city," a man who knew
His Apocalypse quoted me later that week.
The Scarlet City, he said. All over again. Gone.
Gone in an hour. But who deserved this? These
Were folks with families, folks with mortgages
To pay. You or me in the right place
At the wrong time. Plans put on hold. Forever.

Nurses waiting for patients who never appeared.
A priest saying Mass in the smouldering rubble.
The dead, the many dead, and the millions more
Wounded that morning. Mother of sorrows,
What can I say? Here in my room, I watch you
Watching your son, the one they will crucify
In their own good time, as they crucified him here
At Ground Zero. A mother grieves, while
Her little ones wonder where is their daddy.

And where *are* the lost who paid with their lives?
A mother grieves, and my eye follows hers down
To her child. *Remember*, he says at the omega point
Of the final Book, *Remember this well. I am*
The morning star rising once more above
My beloved city, as above the homes of my Afghans,
Above my whole bent, broken world. Have I not
Told you I will not leave you orphans? Not
One of you. Not one, not a single precious one.

I Did Say Yes

Thou heardst me, truer than tongue, confess . . .
            Gerard Manley Hopkins

The barely prayable prayer as words fall away,
Words unguessed or unguessable, soft silence only,
Penetrant silence, the pit, then something stirring . . .
Importunate, unquenchable mind, astray
Or aswarm, attuned for odd moments after, then
Drifting. Then a lull & a lifting, then self flickering back,
As the parched sunflower turns towards the sun. . . .

A woman kneels, head bent forward, each cell attendant
Upon the flame which, consuming, does not consume,
But gently enwrapts, caressing, filling her self with itself,
The burning clouds lingering, then hovering off, like
Mist off a mountain, here in this kitchen, this cell, here,
Where the timeless crosses with time, this chiasmus,
Infinity & now, nowhere & always, this cosmos, this fresh-

Found dimension, all attention gone over now, as flame
Flickers and whispers, all care turning to ash, all fear,
All consequence even, all given over, ah, lover to lover
Now, saying yes, yes, ah, thy will be done, my dear,
Yes echoing down the long halls of time, yes,
In spite of all disappointment, of the death of Love even,
The barely sayable yes again, yes again, yes I will. Yes.

WEDDING SONG

And so it goes. And so it goes.
The great tree blossoms, leafs, & grows.
Come sun, come moon, come storms, come snows.
So turn our years. And so it goes.

Man meets a woman. And so it goes.
And time runs on, and love's fruit grows.
Through smooth & rough, through highs & lows,
The great tree blossoms, leafs, & grows.

And as time ripens, love likewise grows.
The smiles brighten, the flushed heart glows.
And *yes* each vows above life's blows.
And the roots grow deeper. And so it goes.

Maria, John, dears, the good Lord knows
We wish you joy, years, Jills & Joes.
And wisdom, love, all life bestows.
Where true love blossoms the great tree grows.

For John & Maria on their wedding day, 4 July 1998

79

BIRDSONG

Alone onto the alone he would have gone,
Content to be his own man in all ways.
One who sought solace in woods & bays,
Who bode his time & would not be put upon.

And she was one who went about *her* ways,
Kind & smart & with a love of birds,
Their trebled songs playing to her trebled words,
Mazelike creatures who could not escape her gaze.

A gaze for once that seemed to hold him, the way
Lamplight holds a deer's eyes in its beams
And keeps the deer from going where it only seems
To want to go. Strangely, it was her gentle sway

Alone that could have ever held him, but it did.
He was aware now of another in the grove,
A woman he would come in time to love,
Someone worth bidding for, as he would bid.

For Mark & Karen on their wedding Day, 26 June 1999

EPITHALAMION FOR AN OLD FRIEND & A NEW
For Barry Moser & Emily Crowe

An island once there was, susurred by the prospered
sea. And to this island Adam brought his fair-haired Eve
at the summer solstice, towards that first evening.
Or was it Eve who at evening brought her Adam?

Who can say for sure? For by then the two
had metamorphed to one, the brilliant vine
and branches, two halves of that one whole,
the seasons of a life and light and laughter

reflected in what their eyes surveyed, a brave
new world the two of them were every day inventing.
Add in daughters, sons-in-law, and all those golden
grandkids to the mix, and huge dogs too

and God knows what—etchings, drawings, paintings,
books & books galore. Then add the strains of music
to ring the fragrant air. Add friends, of course,
who wished them both beneficence, then add in love

and hope, and the memory of some obscure sacred space
where promises were made and prayer made valid.
Then add the poignant, arrant spice of song,
all brought hither to this ancient island in the sun,

a sun they knew must someday sink into the sea
to meet the fragrant night & rest a while there,
before it rose refreshed the morning after, amidst
a din of dogs & dishes, but washed anew in light.

June 21, 2003
Summer Solstice, Antigua

High Tea with Miss Julianna

'Begin at the beginning,' the King said gravely, 'and go on
till you come to the end: then stop.'

In the land of the JubJub together they had tea.
High tea, one has to understand, six cups of imaginary
tea, the good Miss Julianna Frances, aged two
and a half, and her grandfather, sixty-four. "How *do*
you do this afternoon, Miss Julianna," he began,
good manners there in JubJub Land
being understood and *de rigueur* between
the Professor and his finical little Queen.
Sporting diapers beneath her summer dress,
she poured her airy tea in cups with such finesse
they might've been in Queen Victoria's drawing room
instead of in his modest parlor. "Might I presume
upon you, my lady dear, for yet another piece of cake?"
"Oh, sure," she too demurely said. "But let me bake
it first. It will only take one minute." I.e., one minute
in her understanding, for they had time within it
for another cup or two or four or six or three
of Miss Julianna's very best imaginary tea,
and time for her to sit upon his lap so he might read her
all about the Midnight Land of JubJub and then confer
together about the best way to pick the naughty dirt
from between their toes, or which of her many skirts
her dolly, coincidentally named for Daddy John,
should wear, and which chair he should sit upon
if Daddy John were to be invited to partake

of tea with them, together with a second piece of cake,
which was humming along just fine in the imaginary
oven in the slowly darkening room. High tea
on a Sunday afternoon at summer's end,
sweet credences of summer. How better to spend
an hour, a day, a year? And Alice leading down
the rabbit hole, and him following into JubJub town,
and all cares left behind now, as the little girl—who would
not be little long—beckoned toward the still-enchanted wood.

There Was a Boy Once

There was a boy once went out
to find the world. And the world,
it seems, found him in return.
From what his parents saw, nothing
ever seemed to satisfy the boy.
And as he worked his way toward
manhood, he tried on everything—
knowledge, sports, a two-piece
business suit, a Navy uniform.
He tried on causes, and rode a bike once
all the way from Boston west to Santa Barbara
in the high sirocco winds to feed the hungry.
Likewise he tried on languages:
Spanish first, then Chinese. Even Arabic
with a French accent, and read *The Economist*
and *The New York Times*, and in one long
summer combed all the classics from Gilgamesh
to what he dubbed "those awful Modernists."
Sci Fi by the box, and Merton, and three volumes
on the English Language. Likewise the Bible,
cover to cover, I would add, and once—in Morocco—
the Qu'ran too
                    Somewhere in all of this
he heard God whisper. Perhaps it came when he
was twelve, and asked his parents for Chinese
lessons, the only Caucasian in the class. Perhaps
when—at his confirmation—he took the name Ignatius.
"Ignatius?," the bishop quipped. "There's trouble."

Still, how explain why he followed where he did?
The answer's plain. The answer's complex,
subtle, contradictory, yet finally very plain.
After two years in Taiwan, he landed on the Chinese
coast. Heading north—so the story goes—
and traveling third class with dogs and roosters,
as he neared Beijing, there was the Voice.
"Well, what are you waiting for?" it said,
and may even have called him by his name,
though he surely knew to whom the Voice
was talking. The rest is history. The rest is joining
the Company of Jesus out in California.
The rest is L.A., Fordham, Seattle, Mexico,
and Berkeley. Ditto Hollywood and Chicago, and
wherever else he's called. "I did a practice mass,"
he wrote just before his ordination after eleven years
of study. "And I am happy to say I was as stiff
as the tin man and as adept with the Sacramentary
as with a Sanskrit grammar. I guess I need
a little more practice before they unleash me
on God's people." Once his father also heard
a voice (the family always was a little strange).
"Don't worry about your son," is what he heard.
"You and his mother have taken him this far.
The rest is between him and me." With that peace
settled on the anxious father. A strange place,
this world of Mystery, where things never
seem to add up the way you think they should.
Where for every gift you give, the Lord
increases that a hundred. The proof, they say,

is in the breaking of one self to feed the hungry.
And who among us has not been hungry?
Has not wished for the gnawing void
to be filled with light? A boy went out to
meet the world, and the world met a man,
who understood that for every no
there is a yes if only, like his Master,
he could just say yes and yes and yet again a yes.
And so he took a cup that he would
come to share with others, and on the bottom
wrote: "Ordained to serve." And thus it was
the boy I speak of finally found himself.

For Paul, June 2002

THE CUP

This chalice, made of burnished gold,
when not in use rests in the place
of honor high on our old oak cupboard
in our dining room here in Montague.
A modest thing, the cup, with a small
cross on the base in Chinese red,
in the center of which there rests an even
more modest diamond, which once
adorned the engagement ring I placed
on my wife's fourth finger forty years ago
there among the unicorns sequestered
in the Cloisters, who to this day look out
over the fabled Hudson toward New Jersey.
This was the same ring her girlfriends
used to say was oh so cute and so adorable,
and which seemed to wince under a Long
Island canapé light. And to tell the truth,
I'd be the first to go along with them, though
the ring cost me twelve back-breaking weeks
hauling bales of hay and rank manure
down at Baumann's Day Camp in Merrick
the summer after college, armed with
a degree in English and—except for her
zero prospects for the future. A week
before I left home to begin teaching
in the inhospitable Chenango Valley, we drove
down to Canal Street to a jeweler her father knew,
where we found the biggest diamond
two hundred and twenty bucks could buy.

Understand: I did what I could, and she,
for her part, always made it seem as if
it were enough, love filling the gap
twelve twenties could not supply.
And here's the thing: over the years,
as I learned to make a living, and that
a good one, I used to joke about
the ring, though it strikes me as I tell this
she never did. A year after I bought it
we got married, exchanging vows I surely
tested with the years. In time we watched
our three sons elbow their way into the world,
and saw our eldest enter Loyola's Company
to become at last a priest. And as the time
for ordination loomed, and the awful scandals
broke his heart and ours, she took the little ring
she had for so long treasured to a jeweler's
down in Brooklyn, and had the baby diamond
soldered to the cross there on the cup, a sign
of something good that held against the years,
where now, when the late summer sun
spreads like blood-red wine across the dining
room, it makes the little diamond shine,
until it says straight out whatever diamonds say
in that language only light and diamonds know.

24 August 2002

HOPKINS IN IRELAND

Above the bluebleak priest the brightblue fisher hovers.
The priest notes the book upon the table, the lamp beside the book.
A towering Babel of papers still to grade, and that faraway look
as once more the mind begins to wander. Ah, to creep beneath the covers

of the belled bed beckoning across the room. He stops, recovers,
takes another sip of bitter tea, then winces as he takes another look
at the questions he has posed his students and the twists they took
to cover up their benighted sense of Latin. The fisher hovers

like a lit match closer to him. The windows have all been shut against
the damp black Dublin night. After all these years, his collar chokes
him still, in spite of which he wears it like some outmoded mark
of honor, remembering how his dear Ignatius must have sensed
the same landlocked frustrations. Again he lifts his pen. His strokes
lash out against the dragon din of error. The fisher incandesces in the dark.

For the Jesuit community at Boston College

When We Walked Together
For Eileen

When we walked together
in the cool of the evening,
walked together, you and I,
in the cool of the evening,
after the heat of the day,
after the long hours under the sweating sun,
after the buzzing words like black flies
had at long last ceased their querulous stinging,
after the questions, after the answers
that refused at last to answer anything at all,
in the cool of the evening, when we walked
in the garden, you and I, in the cool of the evening.
When it was no longer important
for either of us to speak, since the words,
whatever words they might have been,
would have been beside the point,
would have said nothing our hearts
did not already know, where simply being there,
there in the cool of the evening
was all that finally mattered,
with the long night coming on, and the last trill
of birdsong fading off in the distance
by the ridge of the tree line,
when we walked together there in the garden,
in the cool of the evening, you and I.

Many of these poems have been published in the following magazines, among others: *Doubletake, Image, America, Pleiades, Inertia, Flannery O'Connor Bulletin, Crazyhorse*, and *The Best Catholic Writing 2004, 2005*.

The typeface used in *Deaths & Transfigurations* is Galliard, designed by Matthew Carter in 1978 based on the Renaissance design of Nicholas Jenson. The book was designed by Barry Moser who also created and engraved the illustrations. The Alpha and Omega devices are reprinted from *Timing Devices*, the first collaboration between Mariani and Moser and published by Pennyroyal Press in 1977. A subsequent trade editon of that collection of poems appeared from David R. Godine, Publisher in 1979.